I was 9 when I committed suicide.

CLAUDE COGNARD

The way I grew up.

I was 9, when I committed suicide

ISBN: 1477659501

ISBN-13: 978-1477659502

DEDICATION

To all my friends, from Facebook and from all over the world.

CHAPTERS

ACKNOWLEDGMENTS

I just would like to thank my parents, who tried to be as good as they could.

My Brothers and sisters whom I do love.

1 CHAPTER.

I do understand those of you, who do believe that males do not know the way they should behave when they are involved with a female. I belong to those males, of course, since I am a man, and although I am neither better nor worse than other ones, I know I am mistakable even when I am in love with a woman, even more when I am in love with a woman…

Whatever our belonging to one sexual category or the other, males or females, we remain stuck to some sort of behavioral and cultural structures pertaining to the cave dweller. What mainly interests us here, are males and their behaviors. In some ways we, males, just act, as baboons would do, relying on notions of strength, domination, experience, supposed knowledge, ignoring what empathy might mean above all, when empathy should concern our female partner, our girl friend, our female clerk, our saleswomen, our manager...

Man has no real knowledge of what it is to be a Man, and they fear they might be described wrongly, when they are just accurately pictured

5

as they are. Today, my question could be the following one. I was brought up in a family, in which a boy was to do what then was considered as task for females.

How did I deal with my feminine part?

What did it become, as I never considered myself as a female or a girl?

Does the upper motivation I had, towards females, arts, literature, friendship, writing, reading, had something to do with machismo. Which part of myself did I stem, deny? I guess that developing both sides, feminine and masculine was some sort of a blessing, which proves whatsoever that we may have been brought up as girls are, and never have become gay, which has nothing to do with education.

Even though some of us, men, may be convinced that they are very capable of withdrawing from old patterns of thinking about women, most of us, still indulge in thinking that men do not have to express their feelings, and that those who do so, are weak or feminine, which leads to suppose that females are weak because they are females. I think I often betrayed my fellow men. I felt guilty about that.

To which extent have I really assumed what I write? I was compelled by my mother to doing lot of works, I hated. Peeling potatoes, cooking, nursing my brothers, sisters, cousins and so on. Changing their dirty clothes. Wasn't I in jail? Wasn't I deprived of my freedom? My freedom is a mental freedom and even today, I can spend hours and hours, in front of the screen of my computer, imagining stories, writing for the theater. Was this loyalty towards my fellow men related to my father? I just wonder. In acting as my mother would do, was I giving up, the parts men had improperly won over women during the years from the very first day, he appeared upon earth. On the other hand I don't like that either, I don't like to cook and clean, as if the fact that I don't do those things made me a man, or why not, turned me into being a more genuine man... I must confess, that when I do some cleaning, I will do it, in the most obsessive manner and that the tiniest trace of dirtiness will be rub away... I've always swung between the pleasure I knew this performance would give rise in my mother's mind, and the displeasure I might feel, in doing it... often, in the end, when I really involved myself in these deeds, this excess in carrying them out gave room to an unexpected liking.

Considering the fact that we live in a society, which mostly think some tasks are men's tasks, whereas some other tasks are considered as women's tasks, I was wondering to which extent, my behaving outside these considerations might affect me and in which way, no matter the Manicheist points of view one may stand for? Obviously, I must admit that I have always understood that these chores are not only men's, and that my questioning is only the consequence of a misconstruction I had got from Parents, who, themselves, had been

brought up under such thoughts. Of course, I

knew, both men and women had the same

responsibilities and obligations at home;

nevertheless, between what we think and what

we do, there might be more than an ocean. Of

course, I may have been entirely aware of all

this, but as far as the context was different, I

may at this time, have chosen, that things were

different also, and this may have involved me,

in a kind of behaving which I still don't perceive

today, and which may conduct me into being a

male chauvinist. Don't you think so?

This is what probably led me to Sartre, and "Les chemins de la liberté", "the way to freedom" which the sole title of, talked to me a lot. Chains? In a play, I am writing one of my characters says. "You should fear all the chains even the baptism ones"." What is the most upsetting for a young boy? Isn't it when his mother keeps on telling him?

"Don't do that."

"Do not accept any sweet, any food, and any game, any...."

A mother who did not ask you if you wanted to

do something, but kept on telling you what you had to do. A mother who, after visiting friends or members of the family, would tell you "Why did you accept this, why did you eat that?". Of course, I know why she kept on telling me, that. She was always afraid that I might take advantage of something that she would not have been in a position to give back, if the ones, who had offered, were to come home. Even today, I have a tendency to be afraid that I might force others to respond in a way they do not wish to. What can I say?

That my mother was feeling inadequate, fearing

13

that she could only give what she had, and she gave me the respectful and honest way to behave, in never taking advantage of other ones. I often trapped myself in situations, where I felt I had taken too much, or not knowing what I may wish other to afford me with. When younger, I was declining all I was proposed and I never measured what was my own territory or the dimensions between my friends and I. To which extent was I allowed asking? What was I allowed to ask? Whom was I allowed to ask for and from?Ever since I got married, I never invited my brothers and sisters, or friends without having a clear consent of my

wife. I felt as if I had no voice, no authorization

to choose, to decide. Of course, I may only say

one thing: It was my own problem and nobody

else's problem, but I feel as if this needed to be

said, as if I needed to make it out, to show it to

myself. I probably was so much anxious that, I

was ready to do anything but put my relations at

stake, and run the risks to be left apart. When

we used to run errant, my mother could leave

me, in front of the shop, because she thought

we would be too numerous inside the shop.

Sometime I could wait for long before she got

out. What disturbed me the most, was the fact that I was not integrated, involved for a while in the family group. I was banned. She left me, as she would have left a part of herself, the part of herself she despised. And today, as she is over eighty, she always tells me that I had been her first baby, that I was the one, she loved the most. I guess how nostalgic she may feel of the time she was a new mother. She shows herself as a loving mother, and tries to touch me. I eschew her attempts and move away from her, incapable of mastering myself. A deep anxiety drives me away; I just cannot bear the idea of

I was 9, when I committed suicide

her touching me.

2 CHAPTER.

Actually, ι may seem tο be explaining things that

ι masterea long ago, ana you may think ι deal

with women in such a perfecι way thaι they all

admire me, in fact, ι'm the man who has tο learn

more than aⅼι the otheι ones. ι spenι more than

halι oι my life, believing ι understooα women,

18

until recently when I realized I had never been aware of them as they really were. I fear I only loved them, when they met my expectations. In addition, what were my expectations? I aimed at being loved, served, helped, entertained, looked upon by any female I crossed, as my mother had always done when I lived at home. Of course, my mother was very talented to do all these tasks, and I was very gifted to take things for granted. You see, even now, I am on the point of telling you, that if I became a macho it is because of women. I would feel more at ease, if I could accuse Adam to be responsible for what I feel and the way i feel it... religion may be at the origin of all this way of thinking, which doesn't belong to me solely. At the beginning, women created an obsequious way of behaving towards males for religious purposes, as though she had to pay for the apple of Eva and Adam forever and ever. Society wants women to believe that they are all weak or imperfect, many women believe that and empower man more than they should and create monsters that no women can handle. Would it be female's entire fault if men are brought up like this? Let's hope that this may change. Religion was the mirror of what I *lived. We had the same constraints same obligation, as in the field of the family, and god who kept a permanent eye upon us. How did I manage out of all this? i do not know. The only thing i know is that i was writing a homework saying: it is not god who created the man, but men who created god.*

My prison was god, was my mother and her obsessional world. I was a very young boy. There was a mirror on the cupboard, and a mirror facing it, on the wall. I do not remember what I had said to my mother, but she turned back to me and smacked me, pretending I had pulled my tongue to her. How can you explain that a mother may strike his son with the flap of her hand, because he pulled his tongue? Whether this may have been true or not, had she to hit me? When I was a kid, I stared at girls as I would have stared at a bear coming out of a forest, although I kept on dreaming of what they could bring to me, as far as feelings could be implicated. I knew nothing, I still know nothing, and I will probably never know anything about female.

3 CHAPTER.

My first genuine step, towards the females, I made it when I started to understand that whoever surrounded me was a screen on which I projected myself. I could only know what was inside my own being, my own soul, and what was different from me, had to be integrated to my own personal sphere, digested and reformulated with my own words, my own culture, my own unconsciousness. What frightened me or attracted me, was myself. Would this mean, we human beings, are all, brothers of Narcissus?

I do not want to draw your attention upon subjects for which I have no space here. Actually, I was an unfortunate boy or a lucky boy, depending the way I look at my own past. I was the eldest in my family, my mother remained at home, and my father shared his time between his work as an engineer, or helping his fellow citizen as a firefighter officer.

Did my father forget to teach me what it was and still is to be a man? he was always absent

24

between work and helping the world ?

I just wonder, if this is not the endless story, of the men who have no man to look up to, got no explanations, but bad role models from a father not loving or respecting a woman.

I felt I was special only for being the eldest...

Sure, he taught me that a woman is a slave to please a man and there is no relationship between women and men apart from superficial ones. He was one of these men, brought up, in families where the eldest deserved more consideration than his brothers deserved, and of course, much more than his sisters

and even than his wife, my mother, deserved.

As my mother still says today, I was his one and only child he has ever carried in his arms. There were no conscious willing from him; this manner of being was so much buried in himself that he never bothered or if he bothered, he never let us understand it.

He was the type of man, wondering why there were no spoons on the table, without the faintest reaction of opening the drawers in the cupboard behind him to get one, or he could ask, if the jag of water would come by itself. Things were to be ready, and the fact that he might be summoned on a fire or on an accident mobilized all the family around him.

I had a first brother 13 months after I was born, a second one 5 years later, my first sister 9 years after, and my youngest sister 16 years later too. As my mother always thought she could do more than what she had to do, regularly, she would invite cousins, or neighbors to look after, and as I was the eldest, I started to do the jobs, I talked about above, which were considered as girls 'jobs. I should say, I was a lucky man, who learnt

27

how to knit, could do some sewing. I could change my brothers and sisters, when necessary, made the washing-up, and I was famous in my whole family, and probably in the whole neighborhood, for my looking after my brother Andre, when Mum gave birth to Jean Jacques. I was five, and I managed to cook and do so many things. The legend is still on, and it will survive as long as my mother will be living.

On one side, thanks to my dad or because of him, I was becoming a perfect macho, and on the other side thanks to my mum, I was becoming what society then, used to consider as unworthy of men. I could not move out of the house. My mother was starting crying as soon as we were to go away without her. As far as my brother Andre was concerned, things seemed easier, she agreed on letting him go, but when it was a question of me, she had many a reason to forbid my going away. My aunt Claire, managed to change my mother's mind and took me away to the place where she lived on the border of Germany, (600 kilometers away from home), where my uncle acted as a doctor. I stayed there for three months, and I felt so well, that I prayed to stay there forever and never come back home.

How was I going to deal with these belongings…?

This is where all story of ass hole, begins. I didn't know I could be one, I behave towards women as a perfect gentleman, I could do a lot for them, I could sacrifice

myself for them, I was ready to die for them… I needed their love, a milky love that as I grew up, became white coffee, and even coffee.

It is a long story…. To be able to show you, how I managed out of assholeness, I have got to be more precise in each steps of my life….

As far as I remember, (let us say, when three or four years), as I sat on the benches of infant schools, I was petrified with admiration for little women sharing my class. I found some of them, so "beautifully beautiful", than I could dream of them, the whole day long, paying no interest to what our teacher was telling us.

Moreover, there will be no end in that...

I was a slave... My soul was belonging to females. I loved them to such a point that no one may imagine how much I loved them, and still love them. I was much too young to get into some sort of intimacy. I could choose one girl to

31

love, and imagine I would spend my all live with her. She became my princess, and she started to live in the depth of my mind. I know that when there is love for all women, there is no real love, but this was not the case, I had made my choice and only life could make me change for another one. I was already becoming histrionic. The young girl was probably the image of an ideal mother, loving, caring... and this could only at this age, be a platonic story. Somewhere I was just like my father was, I was in love with a girl, exactly as my father was in love with my mother, I mean, not connecting with her... I began to consider love as genuine, when It was or

generated idealistic Fantasy. It has no steady

foundations, it was orientated towards unreal.

Sure! I indulged in wishful thinking, I was not in

the earth-to-earth visions of the world, and things

were belonging to unreality, uncertainty and

depending on the power of my mind, on my

mother's mind, my parents' mind. God could

realize all he wanted, and I just had to pray to

get things done. This left me enough time, to

think, to dream, to write, to read.

4 CHAPTER.

I think i have kept much about this way of thinking. Just like these babies who see their mother's womb appearing as soon as they start crying. i will live in this state of mind. Magic!

I could also spend hours doing what I like, since I would just have to pray god, to get things others ones did, done.

My father despised my uncles who were ever so clever artisans; they had gold fingers, and could create anything from a toy to a house. I admired them, but my father thought they had received no education.

My father was unable to make, to confection, to build, to garden, to... What was he capable of doing? I do not know! From my point of view, nothing and I never understood all people who wanted him to come to their home to mend something, repair something else... My father was a clever man, I wouldn't say a loser, just a man who probably never had the opportunity to achieve his goals, to become who he wanted to be, a man that never gave himself the opportunity to achieve his dreams.

I started to write a book about my family. It would be so upsetting for my mother that I keep it on my computer, waiting for the day, no one will be hurt. My father was the only person who managed to make me understand situations, he had just to say one or two words to make me think for hours. He could say things just like "this table is just made of atoms, or of emptiness, or of Nothing".

And this forced my mind to try to find how this could be possible. He used to speak English, in front of my mother and aunts. He was showing off.

When I started English, I really felt passionate, fanatical; I could spend hours studying this language. I still have my first list of words on one of my numerous school notes.

Once I knew a few words, I wanted to check them on him. Dad, what time is it? His answer in French: "You shut up" and words that may not be translated. He became rude and disrespectful, putting me down because he felt

Inadequate, and he didn't want me to see that perhaps his English was not good enough and that I could have noticed that I crossed my whole life thinking he had lied about his ability of speaking some words of English. Until recently, a few months before he dies, he explained to one of my nieces how to say something. It was prodigiously right, and I was very astonished. Nevertheless, I still feel shameful, today, because this has been for me, the occasion to correct what he had said, on a point, which had no serious importance, and I even argued with him. What did I expect then? To be acknowledged by him as someone who knew? Was I expecting, he

might understand I had always been suspicious

about his knowing English? Sure, now, he is

dead, I realize I just wanted to prove him that I

knew English better than he did. He did not

deserve to be treated in such a way, even if I

have said things kindly.

5 CHAPTER.

My father had bought a house, wedged between two other houses. Our door was opening directly on the pavement, a very short pavement, where my brother and I could sit to watch cars passing. This is important because when we were at home, we had no freedom, no space and my mother who had not had the opportunity to attend school, wanted us (her older sons) to do the studies she had never done. She taught us how to read and write before we entered what we call in France, the primary school. We learnt that pleasure was in writing, and when she was vanishing for some hours, probably having coffee with her friends, or running events, we used to have words to write. Later on, we will have to write stories. Neither Andre, my brother, nor I will desert writing. Both of us, still write a lot.

In some ways, we were kept, inside a family

41

womb, home! We had no television, and my father used to come back, so tired that he could not bear us, and my mother used to send us to bed very early, at around 7 o'clock. At this time, the whole family shared the same bedroom, and my brother and I, shared the same bed. My mother wanted us to lay back to back, and naturally, as soon as she had regained the first floor, we started to invent stories, which at the beginning were in relation with fairy tales, I should say, looked like fairy tales, and which gradually involved girls and sexual fantasies.

Something was in mind. My mother always told

us, that there were no differences, sexually speaking between us. This assertion led me to know more about what she declared, and I tried to get some of my girl-cousins undressed. Some of them became my accomplices, and I could not find what deserved to be hidden. When I first step in my primary class, I knew all the teacher was to teach us. In addition, there were no girls, and the only thing I was to do, was paying attention to what was taught. I really get bored, from the very day, I started school, until the very day, I ended it, 15 years later, before my going to England. I imagined I was so good, than I could not bear the idea of making a mistake. I remember a dictation, in which there was the word "giraffe", which is written with a sole "f" in French. I tried to cheat and to transform the two "f", in one single letter. I asked the teacher why He had underlined a mistake where there was none. He demanded that I came to the blackboard, took one my ear, and asked me to confess my trickery in front of my classmates. This signed my total dismissal. From this day on, I only considered my father as the one who could teach me a lesson, whichever it might be. At this time, teachers had no time to squander, in order to find out, if a pupil had particular capacities or not. I was a real lazy and prideful boy, totally inhibited, just incapable of placing one word. The world of men was terrifying, dreadful; I was convinced that someone would kill me. My parents were violent, as most of parents were in the years after the war. My mum could alternate between anger or excessive kindness or remains days and days without saying one word to me. Her silence was the worst violence, and during it, life or even the world had something that looked unbearable. Moreover, she threatened me with my father, telling me that he would correct me when he would be coming back home. She kept

in mind, all the fears she had undergone during

the war, and she was constantly imagining the

worst situations, and asking us to act in the

perspective of a new conflict. My brother Andre,

and I were too young to understand that she was

suffering from depression although we knew that

she had been through a serious nervous

breakdown. She swang between euphoria and

crying endlessly.

The word had something immaterial! The world

was dreadfully threatening, and as far as I

remember, I was thinking of killing myself. I

I was 9, when I committed suicide

wanted to commit suicide. I had no friend in this

life, only my pencil and books that I read and

read again.

6 CHAPTER.

There has been a time during which my mother threatened us of throwing herself and my youngest brother jean Jacques in the river Loire, if we carried on being the naughty boys we were. Her silly desires were mortifying for me. She was killing my soul. I was responsible

for what might happen to her and to my brother.

That was unbearable! She was mentally

disturbed. And no one saw it, and I felt so

ashamed that I would never have dared to talk

to someone about it.

I became an expert in the art of wounding

myself. In addition, my mother used to talk

about my continuous accidents, which for me

now, were pure missed acts, as if I had been

the cleverest boy in the world. She kept on

telling us, (Andre and I), we were ill-disciplined,

mischievous boys and this word is soft, could

49

give us some medicine to make us cooler. The

world frightened me. My only and unique way to

escape, was my mind, books, and writing...

and, when we went to my grand-mother's farm,

because, first of all, she has been the only one

who told me she loved me and because, there

we met cousins, uncles, aunt and my grand-

father.

7 CHAPTER.

I loved the trees, I loved the forest. When my

parents and the rest of the family were there, I

felt free. My parents kept on putting me down,

and my self-esteem was resented, I needed

love and I only received a bad image of myself.

I could hide in the bushes for hours, crossing birds or animals, snakes and so on. We could climb on the branches... Once, it was on 1 January, we had gone to visit my grandparents. I had a new scarf around the neck, and with my brother, despite the frozen mist of the night; I climbed on one of the firs, up to the highest branch. Of course, what was supposed to happen, happened, and I slipped and remained hanged. My father had kept an eye on us, and unhooked me, like a piece of meat in a butcher's shop.

She dealt with us, as she would have done with adults... I have at the bottom of my files, a book about what I lived. Once, I accidentally pulled her knitting down on the floor. She thought I had done it, on purpose; she made me kneel and knocked me, asking me to beg her pardon repeatedly. The more I begged her pardon, the more he was striking me.

She has not been worst than other mothers, she only gave me the ability to write and criticize what hurt me and still hurt my soul and my mind.

8 CHAPTER.

How did all this interfere with my wife?

Beside, did all this had an impact in my relation

with her? The first thing I must say, is that from

the very day, I imagined that someone could

heal my spirit, my mind, my soul, I decided I'd

found the way out of all this. I will not overlook

this aspect of things here. I just want to say,

that I looked for help very soon in my childhood,

and the first book I read, was a book written by

"Young". (This author has nothing to do with

Jung). Title was something like "the strength

of your spirit…" After, reading this "stupid

book", I found a book describing sexualities,

and later on I discovered Freud and when I

came back from England I really wanted to go

through a psychoanalysis. Therefore, I went to

see a Freudian therapist. If I want to be honest,

before all that, I had gone through difficult

relationships with the girls I loved. I had got engaged to Karen, a beautiful girl, while I was in England. I remember how much I stuck to her. I was some real glue, a genuine pot of jam. As my mother had always prohibited me from helping myself when I was at someone home, I dare not act, eat; take food if Karen did not tell me to do so. Nevertheless, what must have been the most unbearable to her was the fact that as soon as we were out of her house, I was scolding her, and asking her why she had not invited me to take food, take drinks and so on. Let us come back to my wife.

It seems obvious, that I just chose the wife who suited my unconscious. First, my mother in law, who loves me today, hated me for more than 34 years. This means that she only started loving me, recently when she realized that I could drive her to her sister's home whenever she wanted. In fact, she was using me. This is very important and I do see the link between this notion and my mother. Of course, I do not want to judge my mother. It is neither my job, nor my desire, but I'd just like to tell what could help others to get out of anxiety, anguish.

My mother wanted to control us, as if we had

57

been water, vanishing through her fingers.

Things were never clear; she used to apply

prepared phrases to make us do something.

Instead of saying, "do this", she invented

stories to frighten us when very young or to

cheat us, when we were teenagers. Instead of

saying that she feared that we (her children)

might engage ourselves in doing thing that

might put our life at stake. She created

examples which she displayed in front of our

young imaginations. My mother had a lot of

issues and my father too. Both of them, were

ignorant of that, and couldn't choose a way to

help me and probably to help my sisters and

brothers. I think that all are allowed to judge

our parents, when what they have done, has

had a hurtful impact upon our lives. The parents

whom I speak about, belongs to the past. After

this digression, let us come back to what I was

saying about women. Undeniably, I acted

towards women as If they were going to mislead

me, or take advantage of me, use me, although

I was always ready to act for them, to perform

anything for them as soon as they asked for it.

Of course, old women loved and still love me,

customers too, people with problems adore me,

I perfectly know how to reassure them after listening to them, feeding them back. I resent that because I want to be honest with everyone, I u want to say what I want. I don't want to validate anybody, but I can't resist to try to look right and be liked by others. I guess this look as passive aggressiveness, I had not found the way to show my real feelings. The fact is that I must take more distance from what my introspection makes me understand, and the way I may act. No sorry, I mean, I must get more involved in what I may be becoming aware of. Recently, I sensed that what I had discovered with my analysts, had been stocked

in a "box" kept in a corner of my mind, in which

I had piled everything. I knew them all, I could

understand what other ones could say, but I

could also overlook the true meaning or what

should I say... how could I say? As, a man, I

had realized that I had removed material out of

my mind, I said "Oh yes, this was the way I

behaved, when young!" I noticed that I carried

on acting in the same way. I know I could

have changed the situation changed my

behavior and I haven't , as if there were no

good at changing, as if my interest was to forget

I could change, as if I said this is bad – full stop ! And just leave things how they are. I know the way, I am the way, but I overlook all this, I ignore all this. Did I overlook voluntarily myself, because I did not want to run the risk of breaking what I had built, within my family or my own job, my own friends? What have I aimed at, through my whole life? I remember, while I was working in the Brighton Chest hospital, one of the charge nurses, used to say "We know the wolf we have, we never know the wolf we will have". She referred to human beings, or members of her staff, but I think this sentence might suit my way of thinking. I changed, but I

never accepted to brutalize the world around

me. I master unconscious to a point that makes

me see clearly what other have in mind or what

they are. As my psychologist said, In fact, I

always fear one thing, I am afraid of taking the

place of someone else. This might lead me to

say, "I have not solved" my Oedipus complex

and style want to challenge with my father.

"Peut-être" ! Perhaps! The problem for people

dealing with me, is that I have to be careful of

...what should I say?   The word dealing is

inappropriate.   Dealing   means   that   two

negotiators are exchanging ideas and trying to find a common ground on which they may obtain a settlement; It would be truer, if I spoke about an appointment with a CEO. It does not take me long to start questioning my interlocutor and to lead the conversation, as if I were the CEO myself. As I write this, I realize also that this may also be part of what my parents were used to telling me. "Stay at your own place". "Don' t interfere with what we say or do or…". Which, of course, I could not have understood at this time, since they treated me as a trustee, the one they could confide in. This had not only bad effects upon my occupation. On the contrary, I was employed to open the first jewelry of a chain store, because of my abilities to manage my own shop, my own staff, and later on my capacities to train other teams, write measures and so on.... What we went through here may seem of no real significance. In fact, I consider it as of main importance.

9 CHAPTER.

Before we turn towards something different I just would like to add some memories, which gave rise to the most unbearable anxiety, and this long after what generated it, occurred. Unfortunately, for my mother, I was enuretic and suffered, if I dare say from enuresis until the age of nine. I was five or 6 years old, when one night, my mother came up to the bedroom, and tied my penis with a ribbon. (Blue or pink,

these ribbons used in commerce to wrap the gift

you chose). I probably felt asleep, for a while

and I saw her coming back and free me from

this stupid ribbon. Did my father tell her that she

was stupid and dangerous? I will never know,

and I will never ask her for this information,

which she would not give anyhow. When my

children were born, this recollection invaded my

mind tinted with an unlimited anxiety, a fear that

embraces all my future generation. I realized

that if my mother had let me the whole night

through with this ribbon, she might have killed

my two sons. This has terrified me for years. I

never told any psychologist ...   There are other

things, which I will probably never dare say...

10 CHAPTER.

I don't know, if I may be good to anyone. Yes, I

once, had the feeling to be good to some

people. It was while I had worked in the

Bevendean Chest Hospital. I really felt in love with my patients. I nursed them, cleaned them, even after their death. I still remember their names. One of them, who had been moved from my ward to another ward, asked the staff to fetch me, as he was on the threshold of death. I remember an old woman, calling me "Christ, you are the Christ !"; I remember Rita Somer, an old woman so big, that we had to be two or three to take her in her bath. Her breast was so long and... Love is a sentiment I was afraid of. When someone shew love to me, I start to think he is going to take advantage of me, try to manipulate me, in fact just the way my mother did it. I know this mustn't be the case I was coming to my parents in law every evening, taking my wife to be, out in my car. My wife was so scared of her own mother that she dare not tell her that we had planned to marry, and this piece of information was relayed by one of her aunt, who had met my mother. This gave rise to a verbal conflict between my wife's mother and I. I told her that if she had not been so frightening she would have been the first one to learn that her daughter anted to marry me. My wife was 19, when we got married. Of course, my mother in law wanted a doctor, a lawyer, someone with a brilliant occupation. My psychoanalyst had warned me that as I was engaged with him, I should postpone marrying her. I didn't listen to him. I never listened to anyone, but myself. At least it is what I imagine. I knew he was right, but I decided not to listen to him. My wife has been a very good spouse. Sometime she may be in a bad mood and change her mind without notice. She has been a good mother, very steady, looking closely at what my two sons were doing and learning. They chose what they wanted to become and they seem happy doing it. I was a

manager, and I probably had not enough time

to share with them, but I spent a lot of time

reading them fairy tales, or stories, riding bike

and taking them to Judo or anything they

wanted. However, sometime, When I lost my

job, it's been very hard for my wife, but she

took time to talk and drove me in the country,

where I probably repeated things again and

again. She hides what she feels, and says

simple words not beign conscious, that she

hurts or upsets me. She may say "Why haven't

I married a man who could do the cooking,

could paint the wall, change the wall paper,

mend.... Etc... or a civil servant, who would

have lot of time to share with me? Or... or... or

a man, with a much simpler mind, not always

trying to think and think over again". I feel

hostile to what I had been forced to doing by

my mother. If I cooked, I do not really mind if it

will be appreciated, liked. I cooked for seven

persons, although we are only two. I can spend

hours and hours writing a letter, a text. I know

that for some women, I'd do all I could. She live

in a world I never visited and I live in a world

she never went into even though we really

enjoyed each other sexually. It's been hard for

her, to accept the idea of all these females I

phoned to, I spoke to, in the company of whom,

I travelled professionally most of the time. I

needed them, because my wife never

understood I might like writing, I might broach

subjects about philosophy or psychology, or

education or poetry... I have always been true

to her. Incredible! Let's come back to stories

belonging to my past. In schools, then, the day

off, was on Thursday. She took the habit to

send us to my grand-mother's farm. I was in

charge of my brother, crossing the town to get

the bus in the town center. I established myself,

in a, how could I say, in a particular state. I was

a spectator of what was going on, around me. I

read and read, and read and read, any books,

any type of magazines, all I could find. My aunt

used to bring tabloid, dealing with astrology,

psychology and so on. When I had nothing to

read, I could put my ear against the radio set

and listen what was on. My life was a sort of

permanent fear. I was haunted by the dread

that my father might die on a fire intervention or

at work. This was in each cell, which belonged

to my body.   Apprehension   is   the worst

companion to live with ....it kills

your spirit and your ability to be free and

choose right, fear is jail. in addition, destroyed

me physically. As a teenager, the first girl I met

was Martine. She was a beautiful fair-haired

girl, who used to come to the swimming pool.

She kissed me on the lips, with no warning, for

the naïve boy I was, if I dare say. I strode

away, and she said; "Oh, sorry, if this upset

you, forget it". I kissed her back, saying; on the

contrary, let' s kiss again!". This very strange

reaction remains stuck in my mind as If I had

been shameful, as If I''d have thrown myself on

her, raped her. I was about 16. Her lips had left

love upon my lips, and I had wished I could

have isolated this first contact to keep it, for my

entire life. I got out of the swimming pool, rode

my bike home, and looked for my mother, to

whom I said nothing, but from whom I would

have wished more understanding, foreseeing. I

never thought this girl was looking for love, as

much as she was intended to give love. I dived

from the border of the swimming pool, where

there was less water, and although I was quite

trained for this kind of diving exercise, I cut my

lips; Martine nursed me, and my heart was

77

revolved, upset, miraculously upset. With Gerard, one of my friends, we decided to take our bikes and ride the 15 kilometers from our home to the place where Martine and her friend came for the holidays. The only person we talked to, in this village, was the bartender who served us a coffee, and we justrode our bicyles in front of the house that we imagined Martine was living in. 2 or 3 years later, Martine, will write a letter to me, when she learnt that I was working in the Bevendean Chest Hospital of Brighton in England, she asked me if I had forgotten her and my response was to write back, telling her, I never forgot the women I had made love with. How stupid! Of course, one of my psychologists told me, that she could see in all these descriptions that I wasn't an asshole, I had a kind soul and my position with women was a passive one, like a receiver, someone that doesn't understand But who thought that that little girl would take you to an interesting place. I trust women in some way and I let them guide me to that romantic place where we live when small and young.

11 CHAPTER .

My best girl friend was a tiny student, with an oval face with a permanent smile, I never knew if we were in love or not. Her name was Antoinette. For fun, we exchanged the rings we had, during the breaks, at school and could talk for hours. She had a friend, Marlene, who had told me, that if a man had beautiful eyes and a beautiful smile, this would be enough for her, to accept to become his girl friend. Of course, I

80

thought she was laughing at me. Some years,

ago, I met a costumer who knew Antoinette,

whom I hadn' t seen for 35 years. This

costumer told me that Antoinette was working in

a town hall. I sent Antoinette a fax and a few

minutes later, she called me. She was so

happy. She spoke about the teddy bear I had

offered her, before leaving France to England;

she said she had never understood my

departure. She added that she had always kept

the teddy bear on her bed, or near her bed,

where I was still today. What did I do, or what

did I say, then? She explained to me, that she

had a very deep religious point of view, that she was involved in priest ordination, and couldn't … what had i said? What couldn't she? Did she imagine I wanted to make love after thirty five years away from her? Did she think I was nostalgic of our youth and that I wanted to live what I hadn't live in her ompany? I don' t know. How many girls did I cross, without the faintest idea of what she might wish or expect from me?

12 CHAPTER.

My psychoanalyst told me, that perhaps I was

so good at showing me soft and easy to guide

perhaps girls thought through my face that they

were more important that really were. I was too

easy to guide, and women do not like men who

let them guide them. This is what crossed my

mind and my analyst said :   That is not true in

that statement there is one missing part and

that is low self esteem women, low self esteem

women are not in peace with their masculine part the taking action part, and to guide your need to be responsible and know what you want. My stay in England will show us how stupid, I was. Brighton is one of the most cosmopolitan town of Great Britain. I collected girls from whom, I could only get frustration and let the ones who probably would have given the purest feeling, go. I always had a girl in my bed. The first one was from Norway. A blond haired girl, with beautiful eyes, she used to go to the Greek school, she and I both worked as nursing auxiliary so as to afford our studies in English.

She was the first girl whom I made love with...

I expected feeling of love from her as much as endless sexual relations. She got fed up with me; I was probably too much fond of her. I thought I had made love! Until I found a German girl, a little older than me, that showed me what making love was. In the meanwhile, I could cross the ways of many a female students, pay her coffees or having meal with. I had to be organized, in order to respect my appointment, and could be with a Italian à 10 o' clock, change for a Norwegian à 12. In my mind, I never thought these girls might have expected something from me. I felt engaged with none of them. Strangely, I could not imagine I could have had several lovers at the same time. This was wholly impossible. I will have to wait for my 50 years old, to understand how awkward I had been, and that this way of behaving was not fair towards them. I remember Maria, a Dutch girl, who used to wake bare foot, all the time. She was a very nice girl, whom I loved being with. Once, my brother, who uses to come to meet me there, met her, and she told him, how unfair I was, and that she didn't understand why, I ignored her; I was more than an asshole. I was a

stupid idiot!   I had never imagined that this

Maria or that all these girls I met may have

wished more than simple talks or walks.... I was

an Asshole! my friend, psychologist told me that

these girls probably loved my indifference and

that this was typical of girls that want what is

not there .I don't think that is assholeness that

is immaturity normal of this age. At the hospital,

among the house keeping staff, there was a

woman, (Gerda), she told me that her daughter

would be pleased if I came to a party, and she

clearly made me understand that Karen would

surely fall in love with me. I had just met, Andrea, an English girl, who was ever so sensitive, so kind... I liked going to the pubs with her, and dancing with her, carrying her and making her whirl around, feet high above the soil, pushing other dancers away and making her laugh. She was probably the only girl who used to come to meet me in my bedroom, without my inviting her. I don't know why, when she came, I took her to the lounge downstairs, as If I were some prude or ingenuous boy. Each Wednesday, after the courses, some of us, took the bus to the town-center, where we had diner. There was a very handsome Suisse-

girl named Claudie, late in the evening I would

accompany her to the house where she was as

an au-pair girl. I never thought or questioned

myself about the fact that a girl might appreciate

my presence and just thought she was happy to

have a friend. Did she want or expect more

from me? Just don' t know! I wasn't capable of

measuring this. The only thing I knew, was that

a normal girl, was to be chased" "hunted" and

would hide what she would feel concerning a

boy, a man. I could hear these females, speak

and I remember them saying: only old men pay

attention to us. (Old men in their minds, were men in the thirties). I gripped the phrases since I still remember some of them, but I was stupid enough to eschew understanding that I might have been involved within those whom they expected to be looked at by.

13 CHAPTER.

I wonder to which extent what an adult has lived in his youth may influence his today' s life. (Stupid question, isn't it?). I will speak of my mother and father, I would like to clearly say that I do not keep any anger against them, and I know that they tried to do all they could to bring me up and the most exemplary way, and that all the mistakes they may have done, contributed to make my qualities. My father was highly estimated, appreciated in the whole city where he gave his time, spare time and so on for the well-being of everyone. He saved many lives, and helped an innumerable quantity of persons. When he died some years ago, firefighters from all ranks and from all the regions came to the funerals. He was a hero, one of those who could have put their life in danger if yours was threatened. My whole life will be shared between unlimited admiration and love on one side, and misunderstanding and the willing of keeping away from him. We probably loved mutually, incapable of expressing our feelings. My mum has been the most rigorous mother, the worst a boy may have wished but she also has been the most incredible woman a man, whether his son or not, may have encountered. She managed with what she had, she became what she has been, always imagining she was a nut, whereas she was probably very clever and lacking of basic education. She thought she was not made for pleasure and that life expected us to work and work and keep on working. Today, after a stroke who had led her to hemiplegia, she keeps on gardening, pulling her stool behind her, and leaning upon stick she asked us (brothers and sisters) to plant in the soil, between ranks of beans or of tomatoes, so as to keep her balance. I said I am happy. Why because I can see the good things of life , the

bright side of change because I am who I want

to be , and I can say yes and no when I mean it

.I am free to be myself .....I embrace my

mistakes and my achievements and I am glad

that I am alive........ Of course, I have always

been aware that unconscious was not to be

despised, that it was in each of us, ready to act

on its own, but when I consider my past, so

many memories seems to arise, that I wonder

what they may conceal, what has been hidden.

For instance, one of my sweetest memories

belongs to one day; I was probably around five

years, which means that my second brother
Jean Jacques was just born. I pretended I had
fallen asleep on a bench in the very tiny kitchen
we used to live in. My father took me in his
arms, up to our bed upstairs. Why have I kept
this memory through my entire life, till now?
Why? Is it because I had cheated and that my
father accepted my deceit? Or hadn't he
noticed my trickery. Did this mean, I expected
him to heed me more?

14 CHAPTER.

Is it normal for a man to listen to women without wanting to put her in his bed? I think I discovered recently that when I was speaking endlessly with a female, she didn't only want to speak even if SHE appreciated to have someone who could pay careful attention to what she wanted to say. It's incredible, isn't it?

For years, I thought a boy and a girl could be

friends, just friends with no sexual expectations.

Am I tricking myself? Was I tricking myself? I

think, now, that I'm over 50 years, that I never

realized that I may have neglected some of my

girl-friends' desires. Even worse than that, I

probably got their sexual desires to arise

without noticing it. Had I got the best way to

seduce girls, without even understanding it? I

became a jewelry manager, and my weakness

as a manager was to accept to become the one

my staff could trust, the one one could tell one'

s life, one' s problems, and one' s difficulties.

Why did I forget what was behind each secret I

had been chosen to listen to, to each character

who decided to trust me? Why did all these

girls trust me? A bit further in this book, I' ll

tell you why my way of thinking became what it

as, and is and which impact this has had and

still has upon my life, whether professional or

familial. …. I told you it was quite unusual for

me to have a girl listening to me. This is not

quite true. My mother used me as her confidant,

her intimate, as far as I can remember. And

the question which crosses my mind today is

why was she inclined to doing this? What did she expect from me ? That I be careful towards her, whereas my father just forgot her. Why did she pour upon me, all the ideas that would cross her own spirit? Why did she consider me as the place where she could dispose of all this matter that was troubling her, bothering her? Was I a rubbish pan? Her rubbish pan? Was I a pure rubbish myself, and she only added her rubbish upon the garbage I was? What did my mother expect from me? That I might be her husband? Are there limits in what a mother may tell her son? Did she share what she told me with my father too? I know she didn't, he wouldn't have listened to her. Was my father fed up with her over boiling sentences, talking... talking talking talking ... always talking, weeping, and complaining? It was not my place to do that. Had she good reasons for her continuous complaining? Of course, if we consider what I just wrote, we may also realize that she framed me as a good listener, a "good ear", (une bonne oreille in French). Did she speak to me because I was her eldest? Or just because I was there, and she could have spoken to any one? Was I just a stagnant mind, being stared at, and she

watched at me, just as she could watch herself

in any mirror wherever she might have found it?

Can you tell me?   I became incapable of

thinking for myself, on my own, without referring

to her, and the best I have ever done all along

my life, I did it for women. When I write this, I

just wonder if it will this be of any interest for

my readers? I don't and will never be satisfied

with what I became. I'll always want more and

more, I'll always desire more perfection... I

want so much perfection that I'll be just what

others might expect from me. I've always been

my worst friend, betraying myself and always ready to make a deal with my enemies, convinced that they were much better than myself, and the worst of all, in this, is that I was sure, that If I wanted to get a little consideration, it was what I had to do. My mother told me about her complicated and intricate relationships with one of her sister. Do you think this is logical for a mother to act in such a way? For instance, she wanted me to be kind, cool, doing all she wanted, and above all, responsible for the good ambiance between my brothers and sisters, cousins or any children present at home, as if I were a chief, a manager, a

leader? I guess, she was only repeating a story

she had experienced. Why not imagine that

when she was growing up her mother used her

as a confidant or perhaps put her in charge of

her brothers and that now, as a mother she

expected that from me. She held me for

responsible and punished me, considering that

if things went astray, as the eldest, I had

something to do with what happened. She could

strike me for that, even when I was not involved

in what was happening. That was pure

ignorance and women at the time were so

neglected emotionally sexually that they begin to be hateful and unfair. It is difficult to give when you do not have. They did not receive enough love respect care and so they did not give it, we us children pay the price. Neglected women became a big problem. That brings me back to situations, during which I wanted to tell what I was feeling to my mother. And she didn't want to listen to me, she started telling me I was a fool, and the more I wanted to say things, the more I felt frustrated, and the more she treated me as a mad boy, insane, "fou", repeating, "Look at him, he is mad ! He is mad". You must understand mad, in the psychiatric way. The only manner for me to get out of this situation, out of her infernal circle, would have been to jump out from the window. I was just like a dog, tied with a chain, and to which she would have thrown stones. She wanted to make me become a real insane boy. Life was not life. Is it normal for a boy to apprehend life and the environment in which he stood as ...what should I say? As a box, a coffin where he has no space left, and from which he could see other ones moving around, without having his own right to move around himself ? But she kept on explaining she had offered my aunt a roof, she had fed her when she was in need, which she brought my cousin up. I knew she exaggerated the situation, and the way she saw her relations between her sister and herself was distorted. What did she expect from me? Did she want me to be better than her sister? Did she expect from me that I never forgot what she was doing for me? Was I in a position to measure, estimate the importance, the deepness of her involvement, of her gift for me? How Could I pay her back? Was I to die for her? That was it; I was to sacrifice myself for her? Death obsessed her; she was from a large family which naturally I knew every detail about. Her youngest brother, whom they called "Little Peter" had died from meningitis and she kept exposing flashes-back of the circumstances of her brother' s death. Do I really know what respect is? I don't think so. I just know one thing; it is that I happen to say to my wife: "You don't respect me!" Someone may step on my toes and I might shout, someone may walk or stroll on my soul, and I don't know if he strides on my respect, I just think I have no right to complain and just the right to understand, or try to. Often friends of mine told me I should have been a priest. I'm always trying to find excuses for those who made a mistake. Today, I can tell my mother what I thinks, whenever I have to say what I think, I just want to be fair. This willing to be fair, is it a way to conceal something such as angriness towards her? My feeling of being fair is more than that, it is guiltiness and protection because Ilove her so I was protecting her from my own anger toward her, I felt guilty to stand up and be firm because in the back of your mind I was not allowed to be me. Still now, sometime, I just keep my mouth closed because she has become an old woman, and she would not be in a position to fight against me, and I' d disturb her for days and nights. Am I sincere with myself? I think I'm, and that it would be of no interest to make her suffer. I keep in mind that life has not always been good to her, and that she had parents who were very tough. But I don't want her to imagine I' m blind to what she did to me. Yesterday, it was Amandine's birthday (My niece); my wife is Amandine's god-mother. Amandine's mother Alice, who is my youngest sister, has a new partner who asked me questions about some of the books

my brother André wrote. He was astounded by

one of the phrases my brother put down in one

of his first book. He wrote that he needed

freedom and that I had always been a weight

for him. This illustrates the way; I react towards

what disturb me, in life. I had read this book,

years ago and yesterday, when I was asked

about the "emprisonment" I had imposed my

brother to live, I realized that he was unfair, and

that I had put this unfairness in a corner of my

mind. As I told the members of my family who

were around the table, we have been brought

up like twins, wearing the same clothes, reading

the same books, sharing the same way of

playing, closed in the same kitchen, discovering

life at the same pace. When I read this, years

ago, why didn't I take my phone to ask him

more explanation? Who did I want to protect?

Him or me? Who was acting like? Was I

playing a role more like a father? Had he

responded to me like I would have done, with a

parent that had never met his needs, that was

and still is part of the same dysfunctional

environment I had lived in. I have always

blamed my mother for everything and I have

alwalys overlooked what my father may or may not have done good or bad for me. When my father was coming back home, on the evening, my mother used to send us to bed, at around 6 :30 pm.. And my brother and I imagined the stories of princesses, kings, young boys and girls. I mean we have always been very close to each other. How can he have betrayed me, and dare write what he wrote ? At 18, I went to live in England. In a first time, we hitchhiked around Great Britain for one month, afterwards he came and stayed with me, at the Bevendean Chest hospital, and never missed one occasion to come back to visit me. He had a car accident, some years ago, and depressing, he called me for help. I have always been my brother's shadow, and most of the time I gave up some of my rights, advantages, pleasures to allow him to meet his own. I used to turn down what my parents offered me, whereas my bother would accept. They never considered that I may have refused because I was convinced my brother would deserve it more than I. Let me use an image. When we had a meal, if something was left and if my mother asked us, if someone wanted it, I always said no, because I thought my father or one of my brother might want it. Later, when I had my first car, although I needed it, one day my brother drove it and had an accident. The car was entirely broken. I had to work hard to get a new one, and there again, taking advantage of my absence, he drove it looking for me, and dive in a waterway, a ditch, and broke the car again. Was I acting like a father or A mother? I made laugh of all this, naturally. I thing I laughed "yellow" as we say in French, which means we pretends to have overcome what bothered us. The truth is, that I feel hateful about that. I was the one he used to show off, the one he could

insult in front of his friends whom he didn' t

want to share with me, as if I were fatally ill and

contagious. When he had problems, whatever

they might have been, or still, may be today, he

calls me and asked me for help, although he

always told me that he has psychologists

around him among his pupils, who will help him.

He acts as my mother did. I' m his towel, a

scarecrow, his confidant, the one who will

always secure him, trying to find the words that

will consolidate his belief in himself. I' m his

rubbish pan. My mother saw him as the boy

who could do what I would never be able to do.

This looks so crazy. Yes, I was the shadow of

my brother, who would probably inherit of all the

proficiencies and know-how of my father, who

clearly showed his esteem or preference for me.

My brother is certainly the man whom I loved

the most and still do, in addition to me, only one

person loves him: My mother.

Is it possible that I started to take to drinking

love whether positive or negative from my

mother? Although she might deny it,

sometimes she took me with her, in her friends

'home and I had coffee, and coffee, has always

symbolized my relation with her. I always drank

a   lot of milk, I had on one side milk, which I

considered as the positive link, nourishment,

between her and me, and the coffee, which was

dark, and I considered as the negative link

between us. I drank oceans of coffee, ever

since then. I like this image, of a breast, which

came up from socializing.   You know what?

What I will say now is engraved in my mind.   I

was in my second year of infant school. I was

probably at the end of my third year of life. Our

teacher, Mademoiselle Thomas[1] had planned

a wedding to be performed at the end of the

year, on a stage. (The exhibition of the end of the school year). I was ever so happy, because she had given me the role of the husband, one of my female-neighbors Christine, was to be my bride on the stage. She was beautiful with her white dress, and I was ever so tall with a top hat. What may have crossed my mother's mind? One afternoon, I saw my mother at school, in the corridor, she called my Schoolmistress... I saw them talking in the corridor. My mother was gesticulating... the conversation was animated... a few minutes later, I saw, my brother André wearing the top hat and the suit I was supposed to wear.

He had my role and he played the role of the husband on stage instead of me. Can a 3 or 4 years boy, prevent her mother from doing this? I was pure shit. My brother scolded my mother, recently about this, which is stupid. He asked her what had motivated her to intervene within the school and she couldn't answer although she did remember the event. Actually, now I don't mind, and as I often tell my sisters our mother is old, and doesn't deserve that you may still feel resentment against her. She did what she thought was the best for us, and if she made mistakes, these mistakes are responsible for some of our qualities. ... I was sure then, that I was a shadow, my brother's shadow, nothing else, and even the shadow of my shadow. Of course, all this, makes me laugh today, but this is still the truth, and my mother continues to carry on in such a way. This remains stuck against my soul, as a chewing gum of betrayal, and today as I write this, also I do not pretend there might be a link, I remember an accident that occurred to me, during this school year. I fell back from my chair against a heavy radiator, I was bleeding a lot, and someone fetched for my mother who was panicking of course and told me off because I was always swinging on my chair. This has been the first wound I will have to support... many others will come. I knew something I was an ugly boy, a stupid boy, a dirty boy always making in his pants, and I belonged to a dim and silly world, from which there were no way to get out. Mistake! I was neither an ugly boy, nor a stupid boy, nor a dirty boy; I was nothing, nothing at all! And this is the beginning. Can these little incidents, which occurred in my early childhood, still have some impacts on today's life? Of course, I know a lot about psychoanalysis, but I never measured to which point theses situations, may have been such as filter put upon my mind in order to alter what I felt or saw, or thought. I was entirely unable to speak spontaneously, the only thing I could do, was looking for what was to be done, in order to have the feeling I could become loved by the ones who surrounded me. Wherever I went, I could do the washing-up, help our host to serve at the table. At the end of the year, firefighters used to have a fair, where all the families would meet. Instead of having fun with girls and boys of my age, I was helping. As if I had condemned myself to be a sort of "Masculine Cendrillon". I was so helpful, that the chief officer wanted to give me an official military rank. I spent most of my life, acting in this way, which made me one of the best salesman, manager and so on.... At least, at the beginning of my relation with others, until they got fed up with someone who was looking at everything, making sure everything was alright. I had been tamed like an animal, a lion, I had the power, but I never used it and thought that fierceness, force was useless, and that the real strength came from the mind... Sure! I could have become a priest.... as far as my link between my mother and I, is concerned. What I write, just underneath, goes in the same direction and probably will generate the same type of interpretation. But, I'd like to add a few situations, I recollect. Is it normal for a mother to share her own preoccupation with her son, when they imply her relationships with her husband, my father? My mother criticized my father and explained how he ill-treated her psychologically, whereas she could also say, how much she loved him; My father never hit her, and she has always wanted to be clear on

that point, but she has been ill-treated by her

parents, this is undeniable. Have all children

who have been ill-treated, ill-treat their own

children, when they become parents. I know,

this is not always the case, but often the case.

She was afraid that my father might go with

another woman, and she confessed me, that

one day as she was crying my father asked her,

what the matter was. And she explained that

her sister had told her that he wanted to get her

in his bed; so my father would have gone to my

aunt home to put things in order, I mean to get

her to more reassuring terms. It is incredible how far this kind of confession could stir me. I could not verbalize what I felt. Somewhere she was asking me to be a judge, someone who could decide for her, somewhere she asked me to be her father, her husband. This kind of conversation was leading me to introspection which I wasn't ready to make. I was strolling like a spirit, a ghost, a human concept made of ideas, subjectivity, fears and anxiety. Not only, my mother was always in or on my back to tell me how I should act or not, but she also asked me to tell how she should behave, and worst of all, how to manage her relation within her own couple. I couldn't bear this idea that my father could be betraying her. He probably never did. What kind of father could do that? And if he did, what would have happened to us? Would I have to take my brothers in charge? My mother had told me that my father had had a love affair with another aunt, before they got married. Do you know what? A part of my life, I tried to figure out who I would have been if my father had married my aunt. Would I have been the same boy? And if my uncle had married my mother? Would I have been my uncle's son or my father's son? And my cousin, the eldest in my uncle's family, would she have been my father's daughter and so on... Why did my aunt let my father down to marry my uncle? Because he was a doctor? My mother wasn't good enough to become a doctor's wife? My father wasn't well enough to get married to my aunt? One of the questions who obsessed me for long is the following one. Thursday was the day off, for all pupils. I remember my mother disappeared, leaving me and my two brothers André and Jean Jacques. She was going to the dentist's. I think she really did, but I never understood why she was going to the dentist on

Thursday, while she could have gone there,

when we were at school. It was still the period

during which, in France, the idea of having a

love partner for a married woman or a married

man made "well-thinking-people" very

resentful. She talked to me endlessly of

complicated stories, the dentist having sex with

one of his patient, the firefighter captain,

incapable of controlling his impulses towards all

those females so impressed by the uniform, and

so on... I'm sorry to say that, my mother was

hysterical. What did a boy; a young boy could

do with this kind of information? Today, she has the same attitude with my youngest sister's children. And sometimes, I tell her, why do you say that to Adrian, this is not a matter of his. I only knew one thing for certain. When she was pouring upon me, her fantasies, her words and verbs, she was becoming very kind to me, and this will forge my character and the art I will develop, in listening to other's problems, and perhaps also a great capacity of inclosing my feelings and my revolt deeply inside myself, far in my soul. I could accept anything from anyone, without a word and rare were those who realized this. My mother kept on saying,

that my aunt, the one she hated so much and

will always hate, (this is only way she found to

keep a contact with her, to love her,) so my

mother kept on explaining that my aunt said I

was an ugly baby, so ugly. And she was trying

to repeat the story. With my mother, you may

never forget what she was complaining about

50 years ago, because she keeps on saying the

same things even today. I heard the story that

my aunt said I was an ugly baby, when I was

born, one or two weeks ago, as we were talking

about my granddaughter who was born in may.

Of course, today, it makes me laugh, and I do not try anymore to explain that most of the babies are rather ugly, in the first days of their lives. As a kid, I considered this as a truth, and I was seeing myself in imagination, as a troll, or rather like the son of Quasimodo. Of course, Quasimodo's son had no reason for being on a stage, for this exhibition offered to parents at the end of the school year, holding the hand of Christine. I never expressed that, but I felt as the opposite side of what my father was, although I wished from the deepest of my soul, to be what he was... My mother used to say he was handsome; I couldn't be his son, since I was the son of Quasimodo. ("I was the son of Quasimodo". This could be a good title for a book?). I was thinking of these boys or girls, who had ugly parents and who finally were very handsome. Ugly added to ugliness could give beauty as a result. My father was clever, I already knew I'd never be, and that only my brother André had got the necessary intellectual, physical, moral luggage that would allow him to become as good, as skillful as our father. I was condemned to unsuccessful; I was condemned to be a looser.... In addition, things will go this way, for a long time. I will be unsuccessful at school, he will succeed .... My parents were rather poor, and of course, I admitted that if there were expenses to make, it would be for my brother. Both of us, we really had pleasure going in for Judo, Andre is today one of the most talented Master in Aikido in the world. He regularly goes to Japan to give lessons there. Our family was living at 40 kilometers from Saint-Etienne (a big suburb: 500 000 inhabitants), where we needed to go at this time, if we wanted to attend courses in martial art. It was too expensive for my parents to pay these lessons for both of us, and in such situation, they never had to say it to me, I used to withdraw myself, silently, calmly, with no protest, no word, no indignation! However, this is another story and another reason at this time, to become even more anxious, afraid, another reason why suicide obsessed me in my very youth. This looks so crazy. Once a rod has been curved, it is hard to put it right again, without taking the risk of breaking it.

Jean Jacques was born on June the 10th 1958. With my brother André, we hadn't noticed any changes with my mother's body. (Consciously speaking of course). When the doctor came, (my mother used to give birth at home) André and I were compelled to wait in the kitchen, and we spontaneously started to shout, we wanted a brother. I still see the perfect picture of the closed door at the bottom of the stairs. As the years passed on, my brother got long hair, and my mother sometimes could call him Suzan. She was so upset that Jean Jacques was a boy that this will transpire through our way of life. A shopkeeper used to deliver goods at home, and he kept on saying that my brother would one day marry his son. I just wonder how Jean

Jacques managed to keep his own sexual identity, got married and had children. What occurred in my mind? I don't know. Why did my mother buy him dolls? She was explaining that dolls were not only for girls, and André had his own doll, named Jacqueline, the feminine for my father's first name, (Jacques), whom she called Jacqueline as a joke. I never had any.... Sexual matters were occupying my mother's mind and she always spoke of our marriage to come, and was willing to make things clear about impossible marriage between members of the same family. What did she do in her own childhood that may have given rise to guiltiness, culpability? I have never understood, and I will never understand.

At school, I was becoming the most stupid pupil in the world. One of my teacher, used to put me out of the classroom, asking me to pass my head under the water tap to wake me up. No one ever saw I was probably depressed. I was 9 years old, when my parents moved from this tiny house to a larger one, with a yard and a garden, and fields around. Things changed a lot. My first sister was born, two months after our arriving in this new house. The situation seemed all right for all of us. We were much stronger and my mother could not ill treat us physically, as she was used to doing it. My aunt, the one my mother always despised had kissed me on the forehead, when I had gone to bed, on the very first day there, and this remains in my mind as an unexpected gift. My sister was born on June 1962 and I jump from the balcony on September 1962. I have not the faintest idea of what happened, and how it happened. There were one of my father's brothers, my aunt, and two cousins at home... I fell from the balcony, on the Saturday, and woke up on the Tuesday morning. The accident in itself could have had no importance to me if my mother, wouldn't have had the need to say I had spent hours shouting and trying to grasp the sky with my hands, a proof that sooner or later I would become a mentally disabled, not hesitating a single second to compare me with a boy we knew, who was really suffering from deep mental handicap. This prospect frightened me. The day, I had this accident, someone in the street warned my parents, and my father took me in his car to the hospital, where I had x-ray, which showed that I had a tiny fissure in the skull. Although I was totally unconscious, my father didn't accept the doctors to keep me at the hospital and I was taken back home. The doctor who was on guard, during this weekend came to see me, but this was terribly disturbing for my parents, who considered him as someone who wanted to make money. (As you know, in France, doctors and hospitals are free). This episode comes regularly in our conversations. And recently my mother was telling how things were managed this day. And my sister realized that my father had had to go to the hospital on his own. My mother only answered, "I couldn't go; I was to look after our guests". Of course, my sister did not admit this answer. How can you have your son, knocked out…, unconscious and not follow him to the doctor's? I wonder. Nothing seemed to have been upset. I could have died. Never mind, I had no value.

15 CHAPTER.

The day of my accident, one of my cousin was to sleep at our home. I remember him, getting to bed right in the middle of the night. I was hearing every thing around me. I remember my mother panicking because she was afraid that my cousin might have lost his way from the town-center to our home. I remember her blinking the outdoor light to draw his attention in case he might have got lost. Of course, I was not in attendance, probably lying on my bed with no will to criticize or analyze the situation, but there was one thing I understood, my mother was paying more attention to my cousin than to my health.   Dead, she would have probably put me, in a corner, in order that my corpse disturbed nobody.

16 CHAPTER.

This falling from the balcony stroke the end of

brilliant school boy I was. I had been good

enough to occupy the first ranks, from the day I

returned at school, after this accident to the end

of the school year, I will be the worst or among

the worst pupils for the rest of my studies. One

day my mother suggested that André might have pushed me. I was so happy to hear that, that I did not lose the opportunity to charge him with that. Recently he asked me if I thought he had pushed me over the wall of the balcony or not. Of course, when I fell, he was showing off in front of the family audience as always. Why then? I just do not know. I remember the minutes before my stupid diving and this lead me to think I wanted someone to pay attention to me. These three days in a state of unconsciousness, taught me that I could stand in a state between the horror of the outside world and the tranquility of my inside life. From this day on, I will love to close my eyes and try to find back the state I had known then. I was dead and wasn't dead. The festival had gone on, the feast had continued as if nothing had happened, and my uncle and aunt had stayed.... When I was called up, in 1973, I was against army and planed a way to get out of military service. I was dismissed after nine months, which was the most stupid thing I could have, obtained, since at the period we were serving during 12 months. What I wanted to say is this: I had left my uniform and was waiting in the corridor, while a high officer (a doctor) was explaining to a lieutenant that I left the army, because of a very high intelligence that made me unsuitable for this kind of life. I kept this in mind and never spoke about it for years. In 1986, I was 33 years old, I had left my job, and had attended a new training as a manager, in a high school. (Technical university). I started to think I had a scarce level of stupidity, and I remember what I had heard in the army, and admitted I might have misunderstood what these two officers were telling, and I had turned it to my advantage. Of course, there were no hurry, for me to find a new job, but I couldn't

bear the idea of being a load, a weight, for my

wife. This was making me more and more

anxious, and I asked the unemployment offices,

If I could know more about my abnormal

intelligence. They sent me to a special service,

who gave me tests for hours, and I really

measured if I was a nut. When the psychologist

met me to communicate the results, she told

me. What I could translate in these words ... A

level of intelligence, much higher than ordinary

people in the verbal field and spatial field. And

she added that I was so hypersensitive, that I

was to be careful, because any stress situation could put me down ... and so on and so on...

Another person there told me "How could education services be stupid enough to let pupils go through their studies without noticing their abilities, and that she have loved to be allowed to make excuses to me, on behaf of education". Because of what had said about my Hypersensitveness, and the stress situations that might put me down, I thought for years, that these tests confirmed I was a cretin! An ass-hole! A weak person. Recently I saw a TV about these children who could suffer because they had a different intelligence, and they

insisted upon the fact that they might be

emotionally weak, and act in way that

disqualified them within a normal group. Even if

I were Einstein, even I were all the world

intelligence put together, what the use If I

couldn't even be what life could have allowed

me to be? After this TV show, I said to myself.

Well, I admit, I may have a verbal intelligence

higher than my ordinary fellow may. If this is the

case, I will prove it through my writings.   First,

I cannot stand up and defend myself. For

instance, when my former president, left the

company to a different staff, I knew they made the wrong choices in the way they managed the business. Customers started to desert, and instead of saying things, I expected them to guess what I thought, what the ex-president solution, was; The new boss did not want to carry on considering customer as a king to whom we were to say yes to each of his whims. Instead of speaking, I was terrified, I hid myself, I disappeared under the soil... I was afraid of being too impressive, I was afraid of the violence that I had been forcing back to the center of my mind all my life, as if the mother I had had during my youth was on the point of

entering here and demand me to behave as I

would have done during my childhood. This

revolt I felt because of my mother, because of

all that led her to treat me as a foolish boy, this

revolt that could lead her to be violent, was

somewhere deeply anchored in my spirit.

Would I become as violent as she had been? I

still wonder. I was afraid of my own anger. That

was an obsessive trait of my personality.

Thinking that I could hurt someone, cannot be

explained. Was it because I was not in touch

with my genuine anger? As far as intelligence is

concerned, I do not care about what the psychologists wrote or said, it made no difference. But concerning the hypersensitivity which could lead me to a behavior that …. They were right! In my relation towards my new manager, I should have known how to present my thinking, how to say things, how to express my opinions, instead of this, I dared not! I remained in my corner watching them as if we were foes, enemies. I turned them to become my enemies… I thought they did not make the necessary efforts to understand me, instead of trying to get myself understood. I thought I had the right answers to any problems occurring, I

thought I had the key inherited from the former

president... I thought I was cleverer than they

were, I thought I was the eldest, the boss was

my father, the company my mother, and all the

females and males, were my sisters and

brothers. I had no means to create my own

business, but I created a schism within the

executive staff, and made it easier for the new

bosses to eliminate the directors who were

following me instead of the real hierarchy. I was

an occult leader, the one who veils himself,

criticizes, and draws other ones to his own

campground. And this will lead me to be fired!

I had to work a lot, not to become a asshole...

You see?

I'll tell you more soon.

TO BE CONTINUED.

FIRST OF ALL, I WISH TO APOLOGIZE, AS I'VE NOT

SUBMITTED

THIS TEXT FOR CORRECTION TO MY AMERICAN

FRIENDS AS I USUALLY DO;

THE FOLLOWING BOOK ARE IN FRENCH ONLY.
THEY WILL BE TRANSLATED SOON

Facebook love, une nouvelle façon d'aimer.
Claude Cognard.
- **Essai** | broché | Apopsix | mars 2012.

Universal spirit, l'esprit universel
Claude Cognard
- **Roman** | broché | Durand-Peyroles | janvier 2011

Tu es trop vieux -
Mise à mort d'un cadre
Claude Cognard
- **Roman** | broché | Durand-Peyroles | avril 2010

Claire, le malheur te va si bien
Claude Cognard
- **Théâtre** | broché | Durand-Peyroles | juin 2009

Sur Amazon :
Sur la route de Jérusalem
Quinqua Kleenex
Sexe magouilles et Harcèlements
La ménopause des sentiments.

I was 9, when I committed suicide

www.ingramcontent.com/pod-product-compliance
Lightning Source LLC
Chambersburg PA
CBHW070017300526
45794CB00001B/346